TAPESTRY OF LIFE - WOVEN IN VERSE

KAMLESH S. KALTARI

TAPESTRY OF LIFE - WOVEN IN VERSE

KAMLESH S. KALTARI

EMBASSY BOOKS

www.embassybooks.in

Tapestry of Life: Woven in Verse © Kamlesh S. Kaltari

First Edition 2023
Published in India by:
Embassy Book Distributors
120, Great Western Building, Maharashtra Chamber of
Commerce Lane, Fort, Mumbai 400 023, India
Tel: (+9122) -30967415, 22819546
Email: info@embassybooks.in
www.embassybooks.in

ISBN: 978-81-19726-72-1

Cover Design by Sonal Churi

Layout and typesetting by Sonal Churi &
Gangaram Dhuri (Brand Soul Creations)

INDEX

NOTE FROM THE AUTHOR

As I share this collection, I express profound gratitude for the support of those who encouraged me to continue writing and embracing the unexpected path of an accidental writer. This being my second book is a testament to the deepening connection I have formed with the written word, a journey of self-discovery and creative evolution that began with my first book *Tenu Main 'Leh' Javanga - Journey of 8 ordinary men.*

In the delightful array of 36 poems within "Tapestry of Life - Woven in Verse," there is one heartfelt Hindi creation titled "एक नई सोच" that graces these pages, not by my hand, but by the pen of a dear friend and gifted poet – Mehavi Lalwani.

Thank you Mehavi for allowing me to use your Hindi poem and entrusting me for creating an English version of the same. Hope I have done justice and retained the essence of your poem in this creative voyage.

As the weaver of this tapestry, I find solace and fulfillment in the realm of verse. Through the ebb and flow of life's challenges and triumphs, I have discovered the power of poetry to heal, to inspire, and to connect with others on a deeply human level. In these poems, I share a part of my soul with you, hoping that you, too, will find moments of recognition and connection in the shared human experience.

ACKNOWLEDGMENTS

In this heartfelt moment of reflection, I find myself overwhelmed with gratitude for the unwavering support, love, and encouragement that my family has showered upon me throughout this literary endeavour.

To my dear parents, Shamlal D. Kaltari and Kavita S. Kaltari, whose belief in my dreams has been an unyielding source of inspiration, thank you for instilling in me the essential values to live life.

To my spouse, Roshni who has been my confidant, my rock, and my guiding light, thank you for being a source of unwavering support in every aspect of my life. Your belief in my abilities, constant encouragement, and understanding has given me the courage to embrace the path of an accidental writer and share my poetic musings with the world.

To my two children, Advika and Gurnek whose innocent eyes have reminded me of the wonder and beauty in the world, thank you for inspiring me to see life with fresh perspectives. Your boundless love and laughter have infused my writing with newfound joy and optimism.

I am grateful to Mr. Ram Ganglani for his constant support, guidance, and blessings along my writing journey.

To my extended family, friends, and well-wishers, thank you for your kind words, your genuine interest, and your unending encouragement. Your presence in my life has brought warmth and meaning to every step of this creative journey.

Thank you Sohin and Aruna of Embassy Books India for their wholehearted support in publishing my book.

As I present "Tapestry of Life - Woven in Verse," my second book, I dedicate it to each and every one of you. Your love and unwavering support have illuminated my path, and your belief in my abilities has emboldened me to embrace the writer within me.

With deepest appreciation and love,

Kamlesh S. Kaltari

POEM 1

REFLECTIONS ON THE PAST

When I saw my reflection in the mirror,
Apart from my skin texture, found one prominent error.
Reflecting on the past, realized what mistakes
I have done for my gain,
And left my close ones with heartbreaks and pain.
Decisions of mine, driven by emotions, weren't very clever,
No regrets, though emotions did sever.
Life is short, though the road may seem too long,
Should I sulk and sing a sad song?

It's tough to stay away from the worldly filth,
Being used to momentary joy,
and then go through one's guilt.
With some emptiness within to deal with,
The soul has realised staying happy is a big myth,
Until it submerges with its source, the creator,
it was always with.

This poem expresses the speaker's reflection on their past mistakes and the impact they had on their relationships. The speaker realizes that their decisions were driven by emotions and not logic, leading to heartbreaks and pain for those close to them. The speaker also reflects on the fleeting nature of happiness and the guilt that comes with it. The poem also touches on the idea that the journey of life is long and difficult, but it's important not to give in to sadness and despair.

The last stanza talks about the soul's quest for happiness and the realization that it's not a myth but a journey to be embarked on. The poem is introspective and reflective in nature and captures a range of emotions.

POEM 2

A PAINFUL TALE OF MY WOUNDED FINGER

In the realm of humor, this tale abides,
Of a finger's journey, its comical sides.
So, let's raise a laugh, for that brave little joe,
A wounded warrior with a hilarious show!

A vital part of the hand, so simple in form,
Upon which every lover dances to charm.
But if it's injured while cutting veggies,
Great trouble arises, causing much unease.

Some adorn it with a ring,
While others, in their recklessness, swing.
Umpires in cricket raise it to end a batsman's play,
And soldiers in war press it, enemies to slay.
Yet, even a warrior like me cannot halt my stride,
On the grand battlefield, where I won't be denied.

Then, the batsman struck the ball with all his might,
As a fielder, I leaped, halting its flight.
My effort was commendable, but the catch slipped away,
Rooted to the ground, the ball soared for a six, and my finger
broke that day.
Sequels were in great fashion, and it was trend of time,
Post-recovery, would I stop? What fate would be mine?
On the cricket field, by the batsman's might,
My finger was wounded again, continuing the painful plight.

This poem is the English translation of the following Hindi poem which was penned by the author originally in Hindi.

दर्द भरी कहानी घायल उंगली की जुबानी

हाथ का एक महत्वपूर्ण अंग ;
सरल था जिसका आकार और रंग ;
जिस पर हर माशूका नचाती अपने आशिक को ;
सब्जी की बजाय अगर यह कट जाए तो बड़ी दिक्कत हो |

कई लोग इसे अंगूठी से संवारते हुए बिगाड़े ;
और कई बिगड़े हुए , इसका इस्तेमाल करते हुए , नाम बिगाड़े ;
क्रिकेट में अंपायर इसे उठाकर बैट्समैन का करदे खेल खत्म ;
और जंग में सिपाही इससे ट्रिगर दबा कर दुश्मन का घोटे दम ;
और मुझ जैसे महावीर मैदान पर रोक न पाए अपने कदम |

फिर क्या था बैट्समैन ने गेंद को ठोका ;
फिल्डर यानी मैंने उछलकर गेंद को रोका ;
कोशिश थी अच्छी पर कैच गया छूट ;
जड़ गया छक्का और उंगली गई टूट |

सीक्कल का जमाना था ;
मैं किधर बाज आने वाला था ;
क्रिकेट के मैदान पर बैट्मैन द्वारा ;
हो गया घायल फिर से मैं दोबारा |

The poem captures a light-hearted and humorous tale about the author's finger, which seems to have a mischievous destiny of its own.

The central event of the poem is the author's finger which initially gets fractured while trying to catch a cricket ball and later gets hurt again, tells us a comical story about the author's brave, but unfortunate, little finger.

POEM 3

CARPE DIEM

(Making the most of the present time and little thought to future)

Free-spirited, I live in the moment and rejoice;

Try taming me, swear it isn't a wise choice.

No surrounding is good enough to settle me at one place;

I am a wanderer, traveling at a varying pace.

Come rain, come sunshine, I'll still make hay;

Tagging along with interesting ones who come my way.

Picking up things along the way, but attachments, no way.

Call me impulsive, a spoilt brat sans any emotions;

Yet, I'll demonstrate a fiery battle against all oppressions.

Socially connected yet prefer heading on solo vacations.

I chase things that give me eternal joy every time;

Mess with me and I'll turn rabble-rouser in no time.

A bad-ass who can get meaner than all the boys;

Many attracted, only a few impressed by my dignity and poise.

Free-spirited, I live in the moment and rejoice,

Not being treated equal and harassed is indeed a bad feeling;

Hypocrisy may not allow it to be acknowledged,

impacting my well-being.

Initially, I may struggle but eventually will

break the glass ceiling.

Failed relationships can't trample my spirit down;

I'll re-start in pursuit of compassion rather than frown.

My passion is ignited by fire and will spread at a rapid pace;

No surrounding is good enough to settle me in one place.

Try taming me, swear it isn't a wise choice;

Free-spirited, I live in the moment and rejoice.

This poem expresses the speaker's free-spirited nature and their desire to live in the present moment. The poem also highlights the speaker's independence, and their reluctance to be tied down to one place or one group of people. The poem also touches on the idea that the speaker is impulsive and independent, and that they are not afraid to stand up for themselves against oppression and injustice.

The poem also talks about the speaker's strong spirit and determination to overcome any obstacles they may face. The poem also speaks about the speaker's attitude towards rel ationships and how they will pursue compassion instead of frowning on failed relationships.

The poem reflects on the idea of living in the moment and enjoying life without any regrets, it also speaks about the speaker's individuality and how they are not easily tamed. It also sheds light on speaker's determination to live in the moment, and to break free from the constraints of society.

POEM 4

ARE YOU HUMAN?

Something easily accessible doesn't excite you;

Discussions turn into arguments,

your point of view, crucial and true.

You are always found running after things that you don't need;

You think it's motivation, but you are driven by greed,

Surrounded by fake people, who won't move

an inch when you bleed.

Leaving simplicity behind, you complicate your life

stuffing unwanted things;

You plunge into the sky without even waiting for wings.

Don't you feel the need to stop when your heart feels the pain;

The least that is expected out of you is to use your brain.

Don't let greed cloud your judgment, and lead you astray;

Simplicity is key, it's never too late to change your way.

The least expected of you, is to use your brain,

Stop and reflect, before causing yourself pain.

The poem emphasizes the importance of taking a moment to reflect on one's actions. The central theme of the poem is greed, which is the negative impact of a desire for material possessions and the need to focus on what is truly important. The last stanza gives a hopeful note and encourages the reader to reflect on their actions and make a change. Overall, tries to capture the negative impact of a desire for material possessions and the need to focus on what is truly important.

POEM 5

MID-LIFE CRISIS

It started with a hankering to do something new,
Adrenaline hit me, and I got adventurous too.

Not paying heed to things that drove me previously,
Developed a new hobby and started exploring an artist in me.
Unable to decide on my future,
which appeared to be in doldrums,
Gained wisdom, when focus shifted, within,
transformed my outcomes.

Took a while to realise, getting selfish is sometimes a must,
Else you'll be left cherishing memories, lone and robust.
Break the shackles, do what you always wanted to,
Embrace life and let your inner child take over you.

Hang in there, enjoy thrilling silence without being sad,
Don't let the mid-life crisis hit you hard, and drive you mad.

This poem captures the speaker's newfound perspective on life and encourages the reader to do the same.

The poem emphasizes on the importance of shifting one's perspective and embracing change. The use of the metaphor "shackles" to describe the feeling of being stuck in a rut is effectively used to convey the central theme of the poem, which is the importance of taking risks and embracing change. The last stanza gives a hopeful note and encourages the reader to embrace life and not let a mid-life crisis bring them down.

POEM 6

A NEW PERSPECTIVE

Time's-up silent listeners, now let our voices rise,
It's time to reveal the truth that was hidden from our eyes.
No longer satisfied with tales already told,
We'll rewrite an epic, with a narrative bold.

No more trials for Sita, grant her peaceful sleep,
In a rejuvenated Ramayana, our spirits leap.
In pursuit of purity and divine grace,
Challenging Ram's actions, we claim our space.

A game of war, a battlefield anew,
With arrows of change, we shall imbue.
Gather the Pandavas, let truth prevail,
In the court of justice, their stories unveil.

Lessons of respect and dignity,
For a world that thrives on equality,
Let's not restrict tolerance teachings, just to daughters,
Let sons and men alike, embrace these waters.

Break free from the illusions we have known,
Adorn not just the body, but the mind that's grown.
With profound thoughts and purity of heart,
Let inner growth be our cherished art.

This poem is the English translation of a Hindi poem "एक नई सोच" penned by my dear friend Mehavi, a woman poet who paints a compelling portrait of empowerment and renewal. "एक नई सोच" ("A New Perspective") invites us to shed the old paradigms and embrace a fresh perspective, where silence is replaced by bold voices, and truth is fearlessly spoken.

In humble recognition of her perspective, I have the joy of artistic collaboration, and have produced the above translation in English.

एक नई सोच

हर बात सुनी, चुपचाप अभी,
खुलेआम आवाज उठाई जाए।
अच्छी बातें हो गईं बहुत,
बुरी बातें भी अब बताई जाएं!

बहुत हो गई सीता की परीक्षा,
अब नई रामायण लिखी जाए।
पवित्रता के इम्तिहान में अब,
वनवासी राम को बिठाया जाए!

फिर से लगाई जाए बाज़ी,
नया दांव अब खेला जाए।
चीरहरण करने को अब,
पांडवों को सभा में लाया जाए!

सहनशीलता की शिक्षा सारी,
सिर्फ बेटियों को ही क्यों दी जाए।
स्त्री सम्मान और सभ्यता के पाठ,
कभी बेटों को भी पढ़ाएं जाए!

समानता की इस आभासी दुनिया से,
अब पर्दा उठाया जाए।
कपड़े, जेवरों से सजाया तन को,
अब दृढ़ विचारों से मन को संवारा जाए!

"एक नई सोच" (*"A New Perspective"*) *celebrates the inherent strength and potential of every soul, irrespective of gender. Through this powerful poem, the poet challenges us to embark on a transformative journey, one that is deeply rooted in equality, compassion, and the celebration of the human spirit.*

POEM 7

TANGLED RELATIONSHIPS

In the haze of childhood memories, I take a glance,
If only I could see the bond of love and
brotherhood by chance.
We used to play and banter in perfect harmony,
If one got hurt, the pain was shared mutually.

Unaware of when we grew up and changed our ways,
Lost in the race of corporate life's relentless maze.
The waves of youth accelerated life's speed,
Caught in conflicts, cracks began to impede.

I believed you were distant, though not truly bound,
Could we not mend the ties, lost and unfound?
Expensive gifts hold no allure, no need for show,
A few loving words, my heart's joy will glow.

I had many reasons to keep our connection intact,
Despite obstacles, I strived to mend the impact.
As long as my smile remains, teardrops at bay,
My yearning to untangle our bond shall never sway.

This poem is the English translation of the following Hindi poem which was penned by the author originally in Hindi.

उलझे से रिश्ते

बचपन की धुंदली यादों में झांक कर देखूं अगर
प्यार भरे भाईचारे का रिश्ता नज़र आता है
नोक झोक में भी तालमेल दीखता था
चोट एक को लगे तो दर्द दूसरे को होता था

पता ही नहीं चला हम कब बड़े होगए
कॉर्पोरेट जीवन की दौड़ में मसरुफ होगए
जवानी की लहर ने ज़िन्दगी की रफ़्तार तेज़ कर दी
फासलों में उलझे रहे और दरार सी पड गयी

मैं सोचता था तुम अपने हो भलेही दूर सही
रिश्ते न निभा पाओ इतने मजबूर तो नहीं
महंगे तोह्फों की न आस है, न तुमसे मंगवाएंगे
प्यार से दो चार बातें करलो, हम इसी में खुश हो जायेंगे

मेरे पास काफी वजह थीं तेरी और न मुड़ने की
इसके बावजूद मैंने खूब कोशिश की फिरसे जुड़ने की
जब तक मेरी मुस्कराहट नम आखों पर हावी होती रहेगी
उलझे रिश्ते सुलझाने की मेरी चाह बनी रहेगी

This poem delves into the bittersweet journey of relationships that evolve into complex and distant connections in adulthood. It reflects on the changes that time brings and the effort required to maintain meaningful relationships as life progresses.

POEM 8

A SECRET CRUSH

Sometimes I just wonder,

Why I used to feel shy, that much?

Now everything has changed down under,

When your image pops up, why do I smile so much?

Nothing seems to have changed as such,

I wish we were still in touch.

I remember trying hard to grab your attention,

Not sighting you would get me a lot of tension.

Smitten, I liked when you glanced at me with those eyes,

Piercing my soul, which you didn't realise.

Past stupidity no longer bothers me so much,

I wish we were still in touch.

You got me very nervous with your presence,

Always casting charm with your cute innocence.

Taking the lead, you borrowed my book,

Seeing you blush, I changed my outlook.

Don't know why I used to feel shy, that much.

I wish we were still in touch.

This poem expresses the speaker's feelings of nostalgia and longing for a past relationship. The speaker reflects on their past feelings of shyness and insecurity and how their feelings have changed over time. The poem also touches on the idea of the speaker being

smitten with the other person and how their presence made the speaker nervous, but also charmed by their innocence. The poem also highlights the speaker's regret over past stupidity and how they would like to reconnect with the other person. The language used is simple and easy to understand and the imagery used is vivid and evocative. The use of repetition of "I wish we were still in touch" adds emphasis on the speaker's longing to reconnect with the other person. The poem is quite powerful and expressive in nature and does a good job of capturing the speaker's feelings of nostalgia and longing for a past relationship.

POEM 9

ETERNAL GRATITUDE: A TRIBUTE TO MOTHER'S LOVE

God, keep my mother forever blessed,

Grant me wisdom to serve her with my best.

May sorrow and hardships stay far away,

May her face shine bright, come what may.

Stayed away from her for so long,

But memories are fresh, vivid, and strong.

As long as life remains, I'll uphold,

Her teachings, in practice, I'll enfold.

Mother, your presence whispers in my core,

A tender touch ignites the strength to explore.

It fuels me with the courage to face any strife,

And emboldens me to conquer life.

Mother, oh what haven't you done for me,

Endured pain, bestowed love endlessly.

You gave me an identity, held my hand,

Guided me right, forgave where I'd errand.

God, keep my mother forever blessed,

Grant me wisdom to serve her with my best.

May sorrow and hardships stay far away,

May her face shine bright, come what may.

This poem is the English translation of the following Hindi poem which was penned by the author originally in Hindi.

प्यारी माँ, मंमाँ

गुरुबाबा, मेरी मंमाँ को हमेशा खुश रखना,
उनकी सेवा कर पाऊं इतनी सद्बुध्दी बक्शाना।
मायूसी और मुश्किलें रहे उनसे सदा दूर,
बरक़रार रहे उनके चहरे का नूर।

बड़े आरसे तक दूर रहा उनसे, पर ताज़्ज़ी हैं यादें,
जब तक है ज़िन्दगी, अमल में लाऊंगा उनकी बातें।
गुरुबाबा उनकी मौजूदगी, आपके होने का एहसास दिलाती है,
माथे पे प्यारा सा स्पर्श उनका,
हर मुश्किल से लड़ने की ऊर्जा दे जाती है।

मंमाँ - आप ने मेरे लिए क्या कुछ नहीं किया,
दर्द सहा, जनम दिआ, बेअंत प्यार दिया,
एक पहचान दी, हमेशा हाथ थामा,
सही दिशा दी और मेरी गलतियों को माफ़ किया।

गुरुबाबा, मेरी मंमाँ को हमेशा खुश रखना,
उनकी सेवा कर पाऊं इतनी सद्बुध्दी बक्शाना।
मायूसी और मुश्किलें रहे उनसे सदा दूर,
बरक़रार रहे उनके चहरे का नूर।

This poem is a heartfelt and touching expression of love and gratitude towards the speaker's mother. It beautifully captures the deep bond and affection between a child and their mother, as well as the profound impact that a mother's love can have on a person's life.

POEM 10

A TIGHT, SOOTHING HUG

Immediately after she left, she messaged asking,
"Have I forgotten something?" her query unmasking.
"Yep, something," he replied with a grin,
"What's that?" she pressed, curiosity within.
"Nothing," he chuckled, playfully unwinding,
A twinkle in his eye, her heart he was binding.

"Wanting you back," he admitted with a gentle sway,
"Missed giving a hug, maybe that's what's left to say."
"Should I return?" she queried, considering the plea,
"Yes, you can," he affirmed, his voice full and free.
Midway blushing, she turned without a word,
Their connection undeniable, feelings stirred.

A hug they shared, a bond tightly weaved,
In that embrace, all doubt was relieved.
Warmth filled the air as hearts intertwined,
Past and worries dissolved, a love undefined.

Alive in each other's presence they feel,
Promising a love that's strong as steel.
Their hug, a symbol of a bond that's true,
Sealing their destiny, a love ever new.

They knew in that moment, fate's gentle tether,

Meant to be together, now and forever.

In each other's arms, they find their home,

An unbreakable bond, forever to roam.

This poem conveys the emotions of longing and missing someone through the use of dialogue between the two characters.

The emotions of love and the power of a hug to strengthen the bond have been captured and the poem ends on a positive note, with the two characters hugging and forgetting everything else in that moment.

POEM 11
LENS OF PERCEPTION

When you want to converse, it's with someone else you engage,

Turning away from me, leaving me in a silent cage.

When there's a task that demands my worth,

Not only do you assign it, but also meet me on the earth.

Oh, how I wish I kept tabs on every word,

Partaking in banter, not feeling unheard.

Then perhaps I'd be on your dial list,

And today, solitude wouldn't persist.

The fault must lie within me, it seems,

For failing to meet your recurring themes.

Or perhaps it's possible you choose not to speak,

Leaving me seated with futile hopes, feeling weak.

This poem is the English translation of the following Hindi poem which was penned by the author originally in Hindi.

दृष्टिकोण

जब बात करनी हो, किसी और से करते हो
और मुझसे मुँह फेर लेते हो,
जब हो कोई काम मेरे लायक तो
बेशक बात के साथ दीदार करवा ते हो,

काश मैं इधर उधर की भी खबरें रखता और चुगलियां करपाता,
तो तुम्हारी डायल लिस्ट में अवल होता और
आज अकेलापन मेहसूस न करता,

कमी मुझ में ही होगी शायद जो मैं हर बार
तुम्हारे काम नहीं आता,
या ऐसा भी तो हो सकता है की तुम्हे बात ही न करनी हो,
और मैं बेफिज़ूल हिचकियों की आस लगाये बैठा था।

This poem skillfully captures the emotions of loneliness, longing, and self-doubt in the context of a relationship or interaction. It explores the complexities of communication and the subjective nature of human connections, leaving the reader with a poignant reflection on the intricacies of human relationships.

POEM 12

BATTLE OF HEART AND MIND

Heart and mind in constant strife,
Pain and hurt, a never-ending life.
Efforts made, to set things right,
But all in vain, an endless plight.

Brain chimes in, with a harsh refrain,
"You're stupid," it scoffs, "let me explain."
Priorities shift, treatment must be sought,
Else negative thoughts will drive you distraught.

Loneliness creeps in, loved ones out of view,
Endless love still present, but out of reach, it's true.
In lieu of loneliness, forgiveness is key,
Beauty within, must not be ignored, for our well-being.

Fragile and weak, a sudden break,
Trapped with nowhere to turn, the heart aches.
Why does it matter, the pain still persists,
Brain chides again, "Where's your self-respect claims?

A battle between heart and mind,
Where self-respect is hard to find.

The above poem is a powerful exploration of the inner conflict between the heart and the mind. The poem tries to capture

the feelings of pain, hurt, and loneliness that the speaker is experiencing, as well as the inner dialogue between the heart and the mind. The imagery used in the poem is vivid and evocative, and the poem tries to touch on important themes such as self-respect, priorities, and well-being. The poem concludes with an open-ended question, which makes the reader reflect on the poem's strong representation of inner struggles and the power of self-reflection.

POEM 13

FINDING INNER PEACE

A spiritual journey, with maturity in mind,
Changing ourselves, and being kind.
Accepting others, as they truly are,
Understanding perspectives, near and far.

Learning to let go, and not hold tight,
Dropping expectations, and giving with delight.
Doing for our own peace, and not for show,
Proving nothing, but letting our inner glow.

Seeking no approval, from others we meet,
Comparing ourselves, is no longer a feat.
At peace with ourselves, and content within,
Differentiating needs, from wants to begin.

Material things, no longer bring us cheer,
Happiness within, the true way to be here.
On this spiritual path, maturity we find,
Peace and contentment, in the state of mind.

This poem expresses the idea of a spiritual journey and the importance of maturity in this process. The poem highlights the importance of changing oneself, being kind to others, accepting them as they are, and understanding different perspectives. The poem also emphasizes the importance of learning to let go, dropping expectations, and giving for the sake of giving. The

poem also touches on the idea of seeking inner peace, not seeking approval from others, and not comparing oneself to others. The poem also suggests that material things do not bring happiness and true happiness comes from within.

POEM 14

WALKING THE SPIRITUAL PATH

A journey begins, with a single step,
A path to tread, that's not yet met.
A spiritual path, you have now found,
With an open mind, your feet on solid ground.

Nothing will be static, as you move ahead,
New things to see, new things to be fed.
A change within, as well as around,
A journey of self-discovery has just begun.

Elevated and uplifted, every day,
By the will of the Lord, you'll find your way.
Peace within, to share with all,
Heaven on Earth, is where we'll stand tall.

Continue on, this spiritual quest,
With an open heart, and a peaceful rest.
A great choice, you have made,
On this journey, your spirit will be saved.

Don't let your doubts hold you back,
Take the leap, don't look back.
Your wealth and abundance are waiting,
Welcome it with open arms, no more hesitating.

With your creator by your side,

You'll find peace and a sense of pride.

In the life you've chosen to embrace,

Heaven on Earth, a gift of grace.

So, claim your riches, don't be shy,

Step into the light, and reach for the sky.

Your spiritual journey has only just begun,

With faith and trust, the victory is won.

This poem expresses the idea of a spiritual journey and the importance of maturity in this process. The poem highlights the importance of changing oneself, being kind to others, accepting them as they are, and understanding different perspectives. The poem also emphasizes the importance of learning to let go, dropping expectations, and giving for the sake of giving. The poem also touches on the idea of seeking inner peace, not seeking approval from others, and not comparing oneself to others. The poem also suggests that material things do not bring happiness and true happiness comes from within.

POEM 15

GUIDANCE FROM THE MASTER

A Master's words, to his dear disciple,
Come to me, and the darkness will be brittle.
The meaning of life, will be revealed in due time,
Your doubts and fears, will be left behind.

Effortlessly learn, and understand,
My peace that passes all understanding, will be at hand.
Peace within, will reflect without,
All souls you meet, will have a peaceful bout.

Lift up your heart, with deep love, praise and gratitude,
Go forth this day, with peace, as your attitude.
I've placed you there, to share these gems,
Love, praise, and gratitude, to the world, it seems.

Open your heart, and do it now,
I am watching, take a bow.

To grow in life, you must stretch and go through tests,
You need to be strong, through stresses and stresses.
Relax, place everything in my hands,
I'll guide and direct you, through life's demands.

Have faith, trust in me,

Through the sea of challenges, I'll set you free.

Believe it, you have everything to gain,

With me, all things are possible, let go of your pain.

This poem is about a master imparting wisdom to his disciple. The master encourages the disciple to come to him and the darkness will be brittle, meaning that the true meaning of life will be revealed. The master advises the disciple to leave behind doubts and fears and effortlessly learn and understand the peace that passes all understanding. The master also encourages the disciple to have peace within and to reflect it without, to lift up their heart with deep love, praise, and gratitude, and to go forth this day with peace as attitude. The master also emphasizes the importance of faith and trust in him, and that through the sea of challenges, he will set the disciple free and to believe that all things are possible with him.

POEM 16

THE FORGOTTEN WEALTH

Just think about this, you have money in the bank,
But you haven't bothered to check,
your doubts make you blank.
Forgotten about the riches or don't recall the amount,
Afraid to make withdrawals, not sure what you have found.

You are rich yet suffering lack,
Savings at your disposal, but you never take a crack.
To do something about it, to claim what's yours,
A wonderful spiritual life awaits, open the doors.

The world's riches fade, fleeting and temporary,
True wealth within, your soul's treasury.
Fear and doubts, don't let them hold you near,
Open your heart, let your spiritual journey appear.

Don't let fear hold you back, from what's meant to be,
Step out in faith, and let your blessings set you free.
The Lord will guide your steps, and light your way,
In Him, there's nothing you can't do or say.

So, take a deep breath, and make that move,
The Lord is waiting, with open arms to prove.
That He's got you, and He's got your back,
With Him, you'll never lack.

Connect with your creator, receive all He has for you,

Spend quiet time with Him,

the connection will come through.

Start creating your Heaven on Earth, it's yours to make,

Decide to do it now, for your own sake.

This poem is about recognizing and claiming one's wealth, not the material one but the spiritual wealth, which is the real wealth. It talks about how people often have hidden treasure within themselves (by giving an example of money in the bank) but don't take advantage of it due to doubts and fears. The poem encourages the reader to not let fear hold them back from claiming their riches and starting their spiritual journey. The poem also emphasizes the importance of connecting with the creator and spending quiet time with him, which will help the reader to realize their true wealth and create their own heaven on earth. The poem encourages the reader to take action now, for their own sake.

POEM 17

KITTEN'S TOY MOUSE CHASE

My kitten is running after a toy mouse,

And breaking everything in the house.

She climbed on the table,

But the mouse could not keep her stable.

When she caught it anyhow,

Then she realised it was a toy, Meow!

My kitten's now tired, from all her play,

But she'll be back at it, come what may.

She'll nap for a bit, then start anew,

Chasing that toy mouse, it's what she'll do.

But for now, she's content, with her catch,

Purring in contentment, a happy match

Enjoying her victory, with a well-deserved catnap.

I re-visited a Limerick written by Advika (my 12-year-old daughter) and extended that and completed the 2nd stanza.*

**Limerick = a humorous five-line poem with a rhyme scheme.*

POEM 18

MY ANGEL, MY PRINCESS

Seeing an angel deliver a princess weighing 6 pounds;

I was speechless as my joy knew no bounds.

Grateful to almighty for blessing me with

this profound experience;

You are the very reason for the never-ending smile on my face.

Every time spent doing stupid things with

you becomes special game;

Advika you are very precious, special and unique as your name.

Wishing you laughter, joy and unlimited happiness every day;

Meow - Many Many happy returns of the day !

With each passing year, you'll grow and soar,

Your light will shine brighter, forever more.

May all your dreams come true, my dear,

And may you always know, I am always here.

Happy birthday to my angel, my princess, my shining star,

I love you now and forever, near and far.

I tried to pen down a Birthday Wish for my daughter, who is, a precious blessing for me.

POEM 19

WISDOM OF AGE - EMBRACING CONTENTMENT AND GRATITUDE

The wisdom of age, a precious thing,
Contentment and gratitude, it brings.
We learn to appreciate life's small joys,
The warmth of the sun, a child's laughter, a loved one's voice.

We learn to be content, with what we have,
Not what we lack, for in the end,
It's not possessions, but memories,
That bring us back.

We learn to be grateful, for blessings big and small,
For struggles and hardships, that make us stand tall.

So let us embrace contentment and gratitude,
And live each day, with a thankful attitude.
For it is these gifts that bring peace and serenity,
Guiding us through life's journey, with clarity.

This poem is about the wisdom that comes with age, and how it brings contentment and gratitude. It emphasizes how one learns to appreciate life's small joys and to be content with what they have, rather than focusing on what they lack. The poem also encourages the reader to be grateful for blessings big and small, and to embrace contentment and gratitude as gifts that bring peace and serenity, guiding one through life's journey. The poem encourages the readers to live each day with a thankful attitude.

POEM 20

A NEW DAY,
A NEW
BEGINNING

Yesterday is gone, its story told,
It doesn't matter, it's over, it's old.

Today is here, a brand-new start,
A chance to make it a wonderful heart.

It's up to you to make it shine,
Choose inner peace and contentment to be thine.

Take a moment to be still and feel,
That inner peace, let it be real.

Step out with stability and grace,
Be prepared to embrace the human race.

You've chosen how this day will be,
Make it so, it's destiny.

Why not make it great,
Have a wonderful day, it's never too late.

This poem is about the present moment and how it is a new start, a chance to make today a wonderful day. It encourages the reader to make the most of today, to choose inner peace and contentment, to be still and feel that inner peace, and to step out with stability and grace. The poem emphasizes the importance of taking action in making the day great, and encourages the reader to have a wonderful day, as it is their destiny and fate.

POEM 21

BURNING DESIRE

My heart's aflame, to be with you when known,
I am coming, my craving for you has grown.
Locking lips and curling tongues,
I long to be with you,
You don't know how much I miss you.

My heart's on fire, burning with desire,
With every step, my longing to be with you,
grows even higher.
The touch of your skin, the taste of your lips,
My love for you forever dips.

Whispers of your desires in my ear,
Ignites a fire within, my desire for you, growing dear.
We'll tear off each other's clothes, with urgency and heat,
As we make love, it's a frenzy, a passionate feat.

Longing for you, night and all-day,
I want to experience your touch, your expertise today.
With every kiss and every move, can't let go of the lust,
As we make love, it'll be a moment that forever will last.

In your arms is where I belong,
my love for you forever strong,
In your embrace, my heart's desire, forever long,

Let's lose ourselves in passion's fire,

and forget the world's wrong.

This poem expresses a strong longing and desire for a loved one, the speaker's heart is burning with passion and craving to be together. The speaker describes the intensity of their feelings and expresses a desire for physical intimacy, describing it in vivid detail, with a sense of urgency and passion.

The speaker also expresses a desire to be with this person forever, and to lose themselves in the passion of their love.

POEM 22

LIFE'S MASTERY: A POETIC GUIDE TO ACHIEVING GREATNESS

Life is a skill to be honed with care,
Ground rules and practice lead to mastery, we dare.
Devote ourselves fully and greatness we'll achieve,
Mastery of life, within our grasp, we'll retrieve.

Pay attention to life, don't let it slip away,
Entire decades lost, a tragedy, let's not delay.
Write in a journal, set goals, reflect and learn,
On values, lessons, don't let mistakes go unearned.

Engage in life, give all that you can,
The more you give, the more life will expand.
Set goals, make plans, chase your dreams with might,
Take responsibility, and let life bring new light.

Enjoy the journey, don't take it too seriously,
We're all dust in the end, let's cherish it merrily.
Life is short, let's make the most of it,
Enjoy the ride, don't let it slip.

This poem is about life being a skill that needs to be honed with care, and how by devoting ourselves fully to it, we can achieve greatness. The poem encourages the reader to pay attention to life, to not let it slip away and to engage in life by giving all that they can. The poem also encourages the reader to set goals, make plans, chase their dreams and take responsibility for their life. The poem

also emphasizes the importance of enjoying the journey and not taking life too seriously, as we're all dust in the end. The poem encourages the reader to make the most of their life and enjoy the ride.

POEM 23

PEACEFUL MIND, HAPPY LIFE

Peace and happiness, hand in hand,
Together they walk, on a distant land.

But where does one start, and the other end,
In this mystery, we must comprehend.
We look outside, for a source of cheer,
But true happiness, comes from within here.

It's not the things, that bring us joy,
But the way we think, our inner voice.
We hold others responsible, for our plight,
But it's our mind, that guides the fight.

We must take control, of our own fate,
And learn to master, our inner state.
For when we are at peace, happiness will follow,
And our life will be a masterpiece, to be hollowed.

The outer world, may be good or bad,
But how we react, is the choice we have.
So let us choose peace and take the lead,
And happiness will be our constant need.

We have the power to shape our fate,

And create a life that's truly great.

Let us take care of ourselves, our mind, and soul,

And we'll find a life that's truly whole.

This poem is about the relationship between peace and happiness. It explains that peace and happiness walk hand in hand and that true happiness comes from within. The poem encourages the reader to take control of their own fate by mastering their inner state. The poem also emphasizes that how one reacts to the outer world is a choice and encourages the reader to choose peace, and by doing so, happiness will follow. The poem also encourages the reader to take care of their mind and soul, which will lead to a life that is truly great and whole.

POEM 24

THE KINGDOM WITHIN: EMPOWERING THE SOUL

Is the King in control?

A kingdom without a wise king,
A prince not fit for the throne,
His rule gets ignored,
And his kingdom then left alone.

Chaos and confusion reign,
Foolish decisions made,
The kingdom falls apart,
And control is not regained.

But what if this prince,
Were to study and learn,
From the wise ministers,
And take control in turn?

Just like a kingdom,
Our human faculty is run,
But the true king is the soul,
And it's time for it to come undone.

The mind, ego and senses,
They do not listen to the soul,
And so, the kingdom crumbles,
Out of control, it takes its toll.

But if the soul were to study,

And learn the ways of life,

From the saints and gurus,

It could take back its rightful strife.

For the soul is the source,

Of all happiness and pleasure,

But it's been ignored,

And now it's time to treasure.

So, wake up and look within,

Recognize the ruler of your life,

Empower the soul, Take back control,

And end the constant strife.

The above poem presents an interesting perspective on the concept of control and the role of the soul in our lives. The metaphor of the "kingdom" and the "prince" effectively illustrates the idea that the soul is the true ruler of our human faculty, and that when it is ignored or not properly trained, chaos and confusion can reign. The call to action at the end, "wake up and look within," and "empower the soul," is a powerful message that encourages readers to take control of their lives and make positive changes.

POEM 25

A TRAVELER'S HEART

I find happiness in the unknown,
And my heart becomes a traveler's stone.
Free-flowing wanderlust, if I had the wings to fly,
I wouldn't waste time unearthing treasures, I won't lie.

I feel like a treasure hunter on a quest,
Traveling to new lands, I can attest.
From the mountains to the sea,
Each place is a new discovery.

I long to fly, see the world, unearth treasures untold,
To discover new places, cultures, and stories yet to be told.
The world is vast and so grand,
And traveling it, makes my heart expand.

So let us pack our bags and go,
To places we've yet to know.
For true happiness is on the road,
And the world is our abode.

The poem expresses the longing for adventure and discovery, the speaker's heart is described as a traveler's stone, always seeking new experiences and treasures. The poem paints the picture of a wanderlust soul, who finds happiness in the unknown, and is willing to fly and explore the world, to discover new places, cultures, and stories. The poem concludes with a call to action, inviting the reader to join the journey and pack their bags, and hit the road.

POEM 26

THE LIGHT OF THE LORD

Be accountable, be true,

Act with nothing to hide from view,

Transparent, let Light of the Lord shine through.

Like a child, shed inhibitions free,

Express joy with wild abandon, you'll see,

Your happiness infectious, to all it'll be,

Radiating to those around, let it be.

In your gaze, in your speech,

Let joy shine bright, within your reach,

For happy souls draw all close in reach,

In their presence, joy, they beseech.

Be where you belong, doing what's right,

Joy and freedom will embrace you tight,

Like attracts like, in the Lord's Light,

Best will gather, a harmonious sight,

His Light will guide, day and night.

The poem emphasizes on being accountable, performing actions with transparency, expressing joy and freedom and you will attract positivity and the light of the Lord will shine upon you.

POEM 27

NAVIGATING LEADERSHIP THROUGH MARSHALL GOLDSMITH'S QUOTES

The path to success is not always clear,
But with hard work and perseverance, we shall steer.
Marshall Goldsmith's words of wisdom,
Shall guide us through life's kingdom.

"Successful leaders are willing to admit mistakes,
And learn from them, for goodness' sakes."
"Leadership is not about being in charge,
It's about taking care of those in your charge."

"The best leaders are those most dedicated to serving others,
Their kindness and generosity, like a beacon, it bothers."
"Leadership is a choice, not a rank,
Choose to lead with courage, integrity, and thank."

Let these quotes be our guide,
As we strive for success, side by side.
With determination and motivation,
We shall reach our destination.

The poem is about the importance of hard work, perseverance, and following the wisdom of leadership expert Marshall Goldsmith in achieving success. The message is that successful leaders admit their mistakes and prioritize serving others, rather than being in charge. The poem encourages us to choose to lead with courage, integrity, and gratitude and to use these words of wisdom as a guide in our journey towards success.

POEM 28

TRANSCENDENCE THROUGH TRUST

In every moment, our Lord reminds us,
That the highest good lies within us.
Start each day with this commitment in sight,
Apply goodness to every moment, take flight.

With peace and love, our hearts shall sway,
Radiate to all, brightening the way,
See wholeness, beyond outer guise,
In every human being, our gaze meets, a precious prize.

Reflect on our Lord, in harmony reside,
Chaos disperses, confusion denied.
As we hold this state with glee,
Inner serenity will forever be.

When one door shuts, another ajar,
Expect the best, no matter how far.
Wonders, glories, surprises unfold,
In tune with our Lord's will, stories untold.

Life's canvas we paint, our artistry's decree,
A masterpiece woven, joyful and free.
In our Lord's will, we find our flight,
Possibilities boundless, hearts alight.

The poem encourages the reader to start each day with the commitment to carry goodness and apply it to everything they do throughout the day. It reminds us that we have the highest good within us, and by reflecting and being at one with God, we will attract harmony and beauty into our lives, and chaos and confusion will fly out the window. The poem also encourages us to expect the best in every situation, stay connected with God, and put him first in everything. It suggests that when we do this, life will be wonderful, joyous, and exciting, and anything can happen at any moment if we continue to stay in God's will.

POEM 29

RE-START BUT NEVER QUIT

Dreams and goals we all possess,
Aspirations to achieve, no less.
Obstacles and challenges may arise,
Making us question and cloud our eyes.

But giving up should never be,
For we are capable, as you'll see.
Success is not a straight path,
Twists and turns, a winding math.

Challenges make us stronger, more resilient,
The greatest accomplishments, most difficult.
Don't let fear or doubt hold you back,
Believe in yourself, and get back on track.

Breathe deep, remind yourself,
You are capable, nothing else.
For every step we take, and every breath we draw,
Brings us closer to our dreams, and the life we saw.

So let us rise, with courage in our hearts,
And never let the fear of failure, start,
Always remember that when you reach your destination,
The sweetness of accomplishment is sensational.

With every obstacle, we'll find a way,

To turn the tide, and make it all okay,

For nothing can defeat us, when we're standing tall,

And never giving up, is the key to it all.

So let us strive, and reach for the stars,

And make our dreams, a reality that's ours.

For nothing can defeat us, when we stand as one,

And never giving up, is how we'll get it done.

The poem conveys the message of never giving up and being resilient in the face of obstacles and challenges. It also emphasizes the importance of self-belief and determination in achieving one's goals.

POEM 30

URGENT QUEST FOR SPIRITUAL FULFILLMENT

My soul is in a hurry, counting each year,
Realizing that my future is now quite near,
With less time left than I have lived so far,
I want to make the most of every cherry jar.

I have more past than future,
So, I'll make the most of each day,
Leaving behind mediocrity,
For time is slipping away.

I'll let go of the ego's fire,
Letting go of self-importance, I'll admire,
I've distanced myself from negativity's grip,
And not let it hinder my soul's journey's trip.

I'll surround myself with kind hearts,
Who can laugh at themselves and their own parts,
I'll steer clear of those who think they're above,
With their troubles, self-proclaimed with love.

The essentials are what make life worthwhile,
And that's all I truly need to make me smile,
I'll savor each cherry with intention,
And make the most of every seed and its inception.

So let us live each day with purpose, intent,

Embracing a spiritual adventure that's spent,

For in the end, when life is done,

We'll find peace and rest, you and I, as one.

The poem is focused on the speaker's journey towards spiritual enlightenment and making the most of life's opportunities. It highlights the importance of letting go of negativity, surrounding oneself with positive people, and living each day with intention. The final lines emphasize the ultimate goal of finding peace and rest in the end.

POEM 31

THE PATH OF OPTIMISM

We strive to be optimistic, and aim for the very best,
In all that we do, we put our faith to the test.
With love and intention, our work we shall dedicate,
To our Lord and Creator, His will our hearts dictate.

Let us act with kindness, His love always in our sight,
And do all things with care, with all our might.
Though we may stumble, and need to adjust,
We take a step back, and make the necessary thrust.

For every change, we must remember this truth,
It leads us to better things, and benefits our youth.
So let us be hopeful, and trust in the plan,
For all that unfolds, is for the very best in hand.

The poem encourages optimism and the pursuit of the best in everything one does. It emphasizes dedicating one's work to the Lord with love, intention, and the best of their abilities. The poem highlights the importance of acting with kindness, love, and humility and being open to change and improvement. The poem concludes by encouraging hope and trust in the journey ahead, knowing that every change is for the best.

POEM 32

BLESSED CONNECTIONS

With every breath we take, let's show we care,
To those we meet, and those for whom we're there.
Making them feel valued, cherished, and truly divine,
With high regard, and kindness that's truly kind.

In every interaction, let's show we care,
Leaving a lasting impression, everywhere.
Behaving with grace, so they'll never forget,
That we're special, meeting whom they won't regret.

Let's give our love and show we understand,
And always make them feel like they're at hand.
With dignity and respect, in every space,
We'll create a bond that time can't efface.

Each morning, let's awaken with a grateful heart,
And take a deep breath, and never be apart.
From those we love, who bring us closer to the divine,
And fill our lives with blessings that are truly thine.

The poem encourages treating others with kindness, love, and respect, and making them feel valued and privileged. It highlights the importance of making a positive impression and building strong bonds with others, and expressing gratitude for these relationships. The poem concludes with a reminder to be thankful for the opportunity to connect with others through love and appreciate these blessings.

POEM 33

'ANGER' – THE DESTRUCTIVE FORCE

The intense feeling simmers within, a fire that rages on,
A storm of emotions, a battle to be won.
A force to be reckoned with, an unchained beast,
A wild tempest that cannot be ceased.

Fury engulfs, reason takes flight,
The mind consumed, the soul in plight.
A torrent of words, a vicious attack,
A verbal assault, a venomous quack.

But beneath the flames that roar,
Lies a wounded heart, a hidden sore.
An unhealed pain, a hurt untold,
A sorrow that cannot be consoled.

For anger is a defense we wear,
A shield against a world unfair.
A cry for help, a plea for love,
A desperate call from above.

Let us learn to tame the beast,
To find the calm within the feast.
To listen to the whispers of our heart,
And heal the wounds that keep us apart.

This poem captures the intense emotion of anger, the power, and the intensity of anger and also acknowledges the underlying pain and hurt that often fuels it.

While highlighting the nuances of anger and its impact on the individual and the people around them, it also emphasizes the importance of finding inner peace and healing in order to overcome the destructive force of anger.

POEM 34

MARRIAGE - REVERSE ROLLERCOASTER

Reverse Poem

In this marriage, let love amplify,
Oh, the joy and strife we shall dignify!
With commitment held high, we soar,
Forever cherishing this sacred tie, we adore.

We find solace in love's sweet dance,
A deep connection, heart and mind in a trance.
With light and inclusive stance, we embrace,
Unfolding preferences, not demands, in grace.

In this union, we shall gracefully sway,
Understanding and flexibility guiding our way.
Differences may arise, as they often do,
But love's flame burns brighter, staying true.

Through highs and lows, we ride this ride,
Like rollercoasters at an amusement park, side by side.
Though moments may be scary and unknown,
We choose to enjoy them, together, as our own.

Convenience alone is not our drive,
Commitment and love keep our flame alive.
A divine bond, our marriage we share,
Not for mere convenience, but love we declare.

So let love's harmony lead us day by day,
Through commitment and devotion, we'll never stray.
As husband and wife, united and strong,
Together we belong, in this beautiful lifelong song.

meoP esreveR

Together we belong, in this beautiful lifelong song,
As husband and wife, united and strong.
Through commitment and devotion, we'll never stray,
So let love's harmony lead us day by day.

Not for mere convenience, but love we declare,
A divine bond, our marriage we share.
Commitment and love keep our flame alive,
Convenience alone is not our drive.

We choose to enjoy them, together, as our own,
Though moments may be scary and unknown.
Like rollercoasters at an amusement park, side by side,
Through highs and lows, we ride this ride.

But love's flame burns brighter, staying true,
Differences may arise, as they often do.
Understanding and flexibility guiding our way,
In this union, we shall gracefully sway.

Unfolding preferences, not demands, in grace,
With light and inclusive stance, we embrace.
A deep connection, heart and mind in a trance,
We find solace in love's sweet dance.

Forever cherishing this sacred tie, we adore,
With commitment held high, we soar.
Oh, the joy and strife we shall dignify,
In this marriage, let love amplify!

This is a reverse poem, which is also known as a palindrome poem – that can not only be read in a straightforward manner from top to bottom but it can also be read in **reverse, from bottom to top,** with a different meaning or message.

The reverse poem highlights the deep connection between the couple, the value of understanding and flexibility celebrates the power of love and commitment in a marriage. The poem emphasizes the importance of embracing joy and challenges together while holding onto a strong sense of commitment.

Ultimately, the poem celebrates the unity and strength that comes from a beautiful and lifelong journey together.

POEM 35

UNVEILING LIFE LESSONS FROM THE WALL'S GAME!

In the realm of cricket's grand stage,
Lies wisdom from Dravid's sage.
Lessons learned from his illustrious name,
Now woven together in poetic flame.

Leading by example, a beacon so bright,
Humility, sportsmanship, his guiding light.
With actions, he earned respect and esteem,
A leader, a role model, in every grand scheme.

With focus unwavering, he stood tall,
Mental resilience, the greatest thrall.
Challenges faced, he conquered each one,
Teaching us to rise when the battle's begun.

Together we thrive, in teamwork's embrace,
Respect and collaboration, the foundation we trace.
In building a winning team, strengths intertwine,
Dravid's game, a symphony so divine.

Dedication and discipline, ablaze like a fire,
Hard work and consistency, his truest attire.
In pursuit of success, he never did sway,
Teaching us that greatness is earned every day.

Adapting to roles, with grace he did shift,
Embracing new challenges, a swift and seamless drift.
Perseverance our ally, we'll never back down,
Dravid's legacy reminds us to wear victory's crown.

Courageous decisions, a leader's flair,
Tendulkar's Declaration, a moment rare.
Putting the team before personal glory,
A lesson in selflessness, forever a story.

Conduct unmatched, a gentleman's grace,
In victory or defeat, dignity in every case.
Ethics and integrity, his moral creed,
A lesson in conduct, a virtue we need.

The poem captures the essence of the cricketing idol, Rahul Dravid a.k.a. The Wall's impact, and the valuable life lessons derived from his illustrious career. It emphasizes his leadership, humility, resilience, teamwork, dedication, adaptability, and integrity. The poem tries to paint a vivid picture of the virtues exemplified by Dravid on and off the field. It serves as a reminder of the timeless wisdom and inspiration we can draw from the game of cricket and the remarkable individuals who embody its spirit.

POEM 36

THE TAPESTRY OF HAPPINESS

In the tapestry of life's grand design,
I believe memories, oh so divine,
Hold the key to meaning, to embrace,
Enriching each step, leaving a trace.

Consciously, I choose to spend my days,
Crafting moments in delightful ways,
For it's these treasures I wish to keep,
In my heart's vault, forever deep.

The simple joys, like whispered bliss,
I savor them all, in sweet reminisce,
For when my journey nears its close,
It's these memories that'll soothe and compose.

Like stars that twinkle, memories gleam,
Etching smiles, as if in a dream,
They guide me onward, as time unfolds,
Enriching my story, as it gracefully molds.

With gratitude, I treasure each day,
Creating memories along the way,
For when the final curtain draws near,
I'll cherish the journey, without fear.

As a poet's pen weaves words so fine,

I capture the essence, in each line,

The power of memories, oh so grand,

That adorn our lives, like grains of sand.

The poem captures the essence of cherishing and consciously creating moments that will leave us with happy memories. The recognition of finding joy in the simple things of life and the understanding that it is these memories that will bring us smiles as we journey towards the end is poignant.